Poetry From

The Heart

By

Fiona Pope-Bulling

For whoever appreciates original poetry,
For all that have supported me along my journey.
For my family,
My friends.
I appreciate every single one of you!

Special mentions
Richard Wallis
The love of my life.

My kids
Chris Simmons
Stevie Simmons
Jason Haydney
Jennifer Haydney

Grandkids
Amber Simmons
Finley-Kenza Simmons

All literary works inside this publication were written
and produced by
Fiona Pope-Bulling
Editor Fiona Pope-Bulling
Photography:
Meyer studio, London.
Graphics:
ToonMe
Makeup by:
Natalieswmakeup
you can find more of the work of
Fiona Pope-Bulling on
Instagram
Fiona_pope_bulling
Or Amazon

Love

You, me
Decadent chocolate swirls,
Dipped strawberries with cream
Sensual!

Surround me with your embrace my love
The heart and the mind are but mush,
As pure as a dove.
Words of love trip out of the mouth in a gush.
Tummy butterflies wing their flight when you look at me.
The knees weaken at your touch.
The need of you is intense
Can't you see?
Lie us both down upon the couch,
And rodger each other senseless
Show no relentless.

Sleepless nightmares

Searching for someone who cares,
Emotion, slow motion
Everything's becoming a commotion.
Lockdown, Breakdown,
Days are whooshing by with no crackdown.
I stand still on my feet
But nobody to meet.
Hair is a mess
I must confess.
Hardly recognise the yeti
in the mirror looking back at me.
Oh glory be is that grey hair sprouting from
my chin?
Is this where the elderly look to begin?
Eye brows need a damned good pluck.
Lockdown ends soon with any luck.
I daren't start talking to myself
In fear I may answer myself back and sound
like an elf!
Sorry that a bit Elfist, I know
But it's how I feel right now,
What to do, what to dos
I could push the boat out and build a tower of shoes?
Now I sound like a looney tooner.
All day listening to the radio at some old crooner
Reading this poem back sound quite bonkers
I agree but hey that's me, now ain't that just shonkers?
I had a brain block.
Words of sanity are well out of stock.

The great outdoors awaited my presence
Off I trundled over hills and down the lane,
Far away from my residence.
At one with nature will save me from
going insane.
The lane is narrow
Upcoming car is wide!
Making haste I jumped into the hedgerow
Stingy nettles sting my nether regions I could
have cried!
Covered in foliage I peeled myself from the
hedge.
Sticky green toffee plant, I looked like the
scarecrow
'Worzel Gummidge'
Bees and ants creepy crawled upon my person.
Now sweating my worst perspiration.
Pissed off and sweary words
I stomped off homewords.

I can see clearly now your trouser swell,
Do it to me quickly and all will be well!
Take off your cap!
Don't be like a pigeon in a jock strap.
All this trouble and toil,
I've gone off the boil!
Lost that burning flame.
With your socks left on they are to blame.
Cheerio chookie egg farewell,
Us together will ne'er do!

You bring the lightness from the
darkness,
Let's run away and sing it loud like a
lark.
We can travel near and far,
In our old banger motor car.
Hark the song of the thrush,
As we lie on this blanket hush, hush.
The floral scent that's all about us.
As we give...my dear please don't cuss.
It's just birdie poop upon your butt
There is no need to tut tut!
Don't stop as we lay bare
Keep going like we just don't care.
So close almost there,
Where are you going please do share.
Don't just leave me on the edge
Was just about to fly off that orgasmic
ledge!

Petals swirl and float upon the moonlit
breeze
Fireflies glow their light with the shift of
night.
Everything silent and still,
Wantilda Witch stifles a brewing sneeze
Holding her nose with all her might
She knows it's all going downhill!
Sneezing is never a pretty sight
Always Blow her cat Benny onto his knees
and into the trees,
Wakes up the birds who answers with a
'You woke us up' kind of tweety trill.
Wantilda feels a cold coming on so she takes
flight
Out into the night,
Giving a groggy croak and a swish of magic sleeve,
Off home she went on her broomstick called Bill.

There was an old bloke,
Who wore an old moth eaten cloak
Wisened and cheerful was he,
Into the future he could see,
He saw goodness coming towards him,
Yesterday was quite grim,
He shook his staff of elm wood
Tapped the ground and disappeared
from where he stood,
Life went insane!
Never saw him again.

She held the rainbow in her eyes
Colours of nature refreshed after the rain.
Red are the roses...the colour of lips,
Orange is the setting sun over the ocean
Yellow is the sun giving warmth to her smile.
Green, the emerald that is the grass upon
where she sits.
gazing at the leaves dancing in the trees,
Blue is the lusciousness of the summer sky,
Her eyes of the deepest ocean.
Indigo are the flowers joyful in the gentle breeze.
Violet is the hazy glow of heather shimmering
on the moors on the horizon
This view, right here, right now.
The pot of gold at the end of the rainbow.

Old Mr. Stoggs?
He was claimed to be as mad as a box of frogs!
He sat on top of a mountain of logs.
In his Sunday best togs.
Yesterday he waded through a mile of bogs
Swinging a bag of cuckoo clock cogs.
Today! Well would you believe it!
He rode bareback on one of his best hogs
Down to the shops for a couple of meaty hotdogs.
Yep! Mr. Stoggs was as mad as a box of frogs.

Love is that cloud
That cloud nine where you float
You float after your first kiss
Your first kiss with your first love.
First love is embraced with gentle feelings.
First eyes meeting across the room
gives you the tingle!
The tingle leading you to THE one!
The one tells you of love beginnings
Love beginnings to make you glow with
warmth
Glow with warmth and float on that
dreamy love cloud.

There's a path of gold over yonder.
Where does it lead?
One foot in front of the other and start
to wonder.
The thought and curiosity start to bleed,
There's an upward slope to the left it seems.
The nosiness in me takes over and up I go!
Just go with the flow.
It leads to the edge of dreams.
As far as the eye can see.
Colour. Bright colours everywhere.
A big huge giant ball pool!
I take a run and jump and I dive right
in there.
This is the best, really really cool.
Balls fly in a rainbow all about me.
Oh my!
This beautiful heavenly spherical sea.
I must be away and swim so
Bye bye!

BUDS OF PASSION.

Innocent kiss
The starting point of lust.
Deeper and deeper you fall.
Just a bud that's closed so tight.
It starts to open.
Hands and fingers wonder for adventure.
Petals open and bloom as the passion
starts to flow.

Rock that body to the boogy boogy beat.
Shimmy on down with the rhythmic beat.
Feel it in your heart beat
Get yourself out of that comfy comfy seat.

Swish your booty to the left and to the right.
Wave your hands in the air for all their might.
Dance, dance, dance that's a glorious sight.
Carefree happy body is such a delicious delight.

Sing it loud and make it pop.
Ooh oooh biddly bop, bop, bop.
Let's shatter the rooftop.
Crazy, crazy sing and dance
Woo hoo don't stop!

Oooooh yaaaaaa!

Lights beam in a storm of colour across
the morning horizon.
Hews of every imaginable majesty.
Frothy fingers rise from the depths of the sea
against the cliffs glistening in their magic
touch.
The waves playing with the breeze making
glittery
sparkles with every ripple of the tide.
The sun makes a dramatic entrance
showing its power to the world.
Morning has arrived!

Your that question

That tastes the tip of my tongue.

Ravaging the gymnasium

In my mind!

Spectre of optical

confusion.

Why is that?

You are my

mystery!

Feast

Your eyes

Upon my soul

Feel the heat of

Emotion.

When I'm alone,
I usually think about
the stillness in the silence.
Feeling the softness of the
tranquil air around me.
I close my eyes and float
my mind to another time
another place.
Serenity and peace.

Clouds of steam bellows from my ears.
Caused by homeschooling my little dears.
Blimey O'Riley mate my poor brain
is in a terrible state.
Remembering how to calculate
algebra and equations.
Long ago forgotten quotations and fractions.
My mind is boggling and going cross eyed.
Trying to keep the kids amused and active
I really have tried.
Oh my days! When they went back to school!
The euphoric sense of pent up freedom,
fist pumping the air and celebratory
dancing like a blithering fool.
But then I felt the silence in the house,
Looking around their empty bedrooms
now quiet as a mouse.
Now missing those cheeky little faces.
Mascara tears making blackened traces.
Oh but hang on tho' peace will be shattered
very soon.
When they come home singing
"What's for tea mum?"
tune.

If the world had no colours.
There will be no love.
There will be no life.
There will be no laughter.
No you.
No me.
Believe in the beauty of colour.

I watch

The world

Tick on by

Before my eyes!

If I write a love story,
I would write about two people.
Him looking out to sea under the moon
sending his love with a kiss upon the breeze.
Her lips tingling with the warmth of the suns
kiss brought by that breeze.
The moon and the sun bringing
them together
in thoughts of love.

I looked into the eyes of life,
Everything with wonder
Soaking up everything the eyes
can see.
The glory of the colourful land
set out before me.
I feel blessed.

THE MIGRAINE.

My aura is a tingling mess,
Turning my head into a turmoil of pain.
Twisting like a tornado of jagged
pieces of glass.
Lights of hot mirrors pulsating behind my eyes
then stabbing every part of my mind.
Pieces of my brain contorting as if on a
grotesque roller coaster ride.
My head, on the verge of wild
combustion mercy
in the form of painkillers and a vomit
bowl bringing slow relief.

Tip your love toward the plains of lust.
Kissing your way across my bust.
Walking your fingers south
Making trails with your mouth.
Caressing my soul makes it sing strong.
Baby you can never do wrong,
Hitting the moon and stars so high,
Saying your name as I cry out
with an orgasmic sigh.

THE DREAM CATCHER.

I caught you in my dreams last night,
Your face alight within the weavings
in the circle.
Your smile, wide and free.
The gentleness of your breath in the breeze
through my window.
I felt the warmth of your comforting arms
holding me tight.
It was as though you were still alive
somehow.
A golden glow shone through the
gemstones threaded in the dreamcatcher.
A swish of the feathers and you were
gone with the rise of the sun.

BODY TALK

If my body could talk,
It'd say.
I have curvy bits and am proud of them.
They are part of who I am!
The creases and crinkles have seen
a multitude of life through my years.
Love, hurt, pain, laughter, joy!
I have accepted what makes me me!
So should you!

SMILES ARE FREE!

Shine your smile.

It's contagious.

Light the world

for all.

There are days when I just want
to walk barefoot in the green grass.
Just feel the cool air about me in
the moonlit shower.
Letting the lightness of the dew
caress my skin,
Like a soothing kiss to the soul.

My world is yours

to hold in your arms.

Love me.

Cherish me.

Make me bold.

I wish I could meet you.
But you are hidden away.
Beyond that rainbow
of dreams.
Like the pot of gold
that's untouchable.

Darkness dawns with the awakening
of the night.
Sounds of creatures haunt your
dreams.
The night and the dark where
even shadows shudder.
Evil walks. Evil talks. Evil wakes.
On the prowl for a taste of the earth
of blood.
The blood of life.
The blood of love.

A book reads

between the lines in your mind.

The letters and the words

of the portal to your

imagination.

The molten sun shyly shines,
O'er the thistle strewn meadow.
Life starts popping with spring
colour in its joy.
Today marks the start of new
beginnings with a fresh
new day.

Poetry to me are the words

in my heart seeping through

my pen that I can wholly express.

It keeps me alive anyways

When a tree loses its last leaf
It doesn't sleep!
It is as busy as ever
Seeping up any moisture so the root
can drink.
Replenishing, nourishing, mending.
It stores its inner system of life.
Ready for another round of summer
months to come.

Droplets of breath hung suspended in the
stillness of the night air.
Like the sparkle of dew shining in the
light of the full moon.
Sweat poured off his forehead and
onto the ground.
She fought to catch her breath from
their union of lovemaking.
Sated and full of emotion of them
captured in that sacred moment
just for them.

Sometimes, the night steels,
The waves of desire for you.
To swallow you whole.
Your salty nectar.
Nectar of the gods of heaven.
Ride you until you are broken
from the wild stallion within you.
I can take you into your dreams.
I can mould you into submission.

Walking through the colours of life
with you.
I noticed something that tingled and flew.
The poet in me bloomed
Like a sonic boom.
Bang went something deep inside my soul.
Swallowing me whole.
I felt the love thang
I feel the thump in my heart.
going bang!
Explosions of every colourful hue.
When I am with you.

In the sky the moon shall rise.
You have love,
I can see it in your eyes.
Those feelings they never lie.
You have made me laugh,
You have made me cry,
But the feelings you share
There will never be a goodbye!

The wild wind of need,
Charges through my veins tonight,
To hold on tight for fear of
letting you go.
Lets go with the ebb and
flow of the tide of feelings.
Lets go with the current
and strip us bare.
Let our love flow with a
tidal wave of love.

How I would love to float
in a little boat.
Holding a little parasol of red
That would be so incread!
Watching the wispy clouds
drifting past on their way to somewhere
distant if I could I would be there
in an instant!
But for now,
I Would just be contented just to skim
my fingers through the cool trickly water.
Ooooh yes.
Imagination is what I do best!

Rain.

Falls strong upon the earthly ground
Making wicked huge puddles.
Lovely.
Welly boots made especially for
the best puddle hopping.
Fun!
Squelchy ooozy
muddy mud fun
Making huge great
splashes.
Soaked!

She walked away,
Head held high.
She refused to shed a tear in his presence.
He let her shattered heart slip through his
hurtful fingers.
Those words he'd said tore through her
like a knife through butter.
"I love her, she carries my child!"
Like an echo reverberating around
in her head as she walked away.
She still won't cry.
Can't cry.
Numb.
What he had done.
Can't be undone!

Time shifts fast when
we are together.
Like sand slipping
through the ether.
But...
When our lips touch.
When we meld our bodies together
Time and motion
suspend into another world.
Nothing else matters.
Nowhere else matters.
Just us.

You thread us through the tiptoe
mile.
With our buttercup smiles,
Upon our blanket we do rest.
And feast upon our meadow love fest.
Till dusk we do take our lustful glees.
As we go about it like the birds and the bees.
The clover and the buttercups
have gone shy and off to bed.
But today has been incred!
The time has come to depart
this midnight world now.
Stars and moon in a spectacular show.
Me on the saddle of your bike.
That in itself is a miracle!
I look at you trundle down the lane,
The bumps and saddle hardness
is driving me insane.
I can see a shooting star
above our home.
As we meet the knowing smile
of our garden gnome.

WINDY BLOOMERS.

Washing day arrives again in a hurried blurr.
The events of the day caused quite a stir.
My grans' best bloomers hang on the line for
all to see.
They jostle and billow in the gusty breeze.
Breaking free they fly over the fence with ease.
Over the hill and far away....well next door
actually!
It was rather dramatic as a matter of factually!
The old chap next door spied the frisky long legged
frilly knickers.
With a few tee hees and guffaws and sniggers,
Gran was giving chace with a worried frown,
Running around his garden like a wrinkled up clown.
Tears of mirth came forth,
As the pesky wind picked up speed and
blew for all its worth.
The old chap join the merry old dance
in a jerky instance.
The frilly knickers landed in his head.
The poor old man and gran looked at each
other with embarrassed dread.
Red faced gran claimed back her now soiled
underwear,

Continued from the previous page.

Hurried back home with a nimble flare.
Never again those bloomers will grace the
line on washing day.
As far as the old chap he hadn't laughed
so much since last may!

THE LIFE OF A PENCIL

It's a hard life life being a pencil,
Especially for a writer!
Yeah, being pushed around
morning, noon and night.
So the poetry flows through my lead.
Giving life to words that grow up to be
a lot of words.
A story is born!
Big responsibility for me tho'
Makes me shrink it does!
Everytime I get my head shaved
every few hours making a point.
Then! Then! I get my butt rubbed
on the paper scratching my rear end!
Really wish they would make up their mind
what they are writing!
Yeah! Hard life being a pencil.
Oh well! Such as life hey!

SHACKLED HEART.

The beauty of us from the very, very start,
The moment.
The very moment we met.
Even at the tender age of five.
I've had this shackled heart.
Even now,
So many years later,
I realise it's always been shackled to you!

Roses like ruby wine,
Soft and romantic and so divine
Budded and ready for love,
As pure as the wings of a dove
unfurling petals in the rising sun
with confident delight.
Till the bloom of freedom takes flight.

Flying high upon a windy mile,
Darting here and there wearing a wild smile.
Euphoric cheer running through my veins.
Spying tasty tit bit fishy bits.
I shall eats them for my mains.

I shall croak my caw,
Call to thee my love and wave with
my taloned claw.
Together we shall dance our love in our
feathered nest.

On the eggs I shall sits and wish,
While you find a tasty dish,
I can feel cracking beneath my butt!
Hurry up back dear our kids needs their
open beaks filled up with mushed up fish!

Day turns to glorious dusk.
Scents of earthly dew
and evening musk.
The evening birdy song fills the air.
Murmurations of thousands of starlings.
A spectacular show with such flair.
As sudden as they appeared ,
Off they go to their slumber nests.
Tomorrow they shall rise with
the dawning sky,
And tweet their merry morning song
at their very very best.

Lift your nose to the air.
Take in the wafty smell of the country
if you dare!
Animals in their fields.
Busy tractors tending their yields.
Frolic and stank (walk) up the hill
and down the valley.
Take in the sights as you dilly dally.
Have a picnic by the river.
But with your rubbish into the bin
you shall deliver.
Blow those cobwebs out.
Careful where you tread there
maybe cowpats about.

Hold me tight and fill your boots
with love my darling.
Let us shine that light and feel the
warmth from within our soul.
The universe suspended in time.
Feel the euphoria when the whole
of our being shifted.
When we rock our bodies together.

She shed her tinkly laughter wide.
Like petals in the wind.
Wild and free.
She finds salvation in the smile of the sun.
Quenches her breath with
the rise and fall of the rain
upon the waving tide.
Mother Earth beats her heart with love
for the beauty of the planet.

Pour your heart onto the paper.

Let out your thoughts.

Feel the freedom flow.

Lighten the load babe.

Write and breathe.

When you have that foggy day.
Can't seem to chase the cobwebs away.
Your mind wanders in a dizzy way.
Nerves like cloying clay.
Everything grates on your feng shui.
All you want to do is to hide from the
frey of the day.
Saying "Stop the world, I want to
bet off without delay!"
Or
"Fuck off and go away!"

Great balls of fire juggling in my hand.
You. In a raptured state at my command.
Your quickened breath showing your
imminent release.
The beauty of your face as the need to burst
increases.
Let it flow.
Ride the waves as you let go.

If the sun forgets to rise.

I shall just look at your smile.

It brings out the sunshine.

Swing the moonbeams in a melancholy way,
Glass of some sort of plonk.
That has long emptied.
Thought of yesteryear running through my head.
Making go-karts.
Hide and seek.
Tape recording your favourite tunes.
Your first date, dance and kiss.
Chuckling to yourself into another glass.
Where has the time gone so quickly?
Those moonbeams know everything.

Twinkle twinkle from your eyes.
Looking down from the skies.
Angel wings you shall fly high.
I can feel your breath as you give a sigh.
One day we shall be together again,
Hand in hand we shall fly.

Take a walk through your memories.

Hand in hand with your desires.

Add a splodge of colour.

Enjoy the fruits of life.

Night in with the girls
Bottles of plonk on the go.
Breaking out into endless chatter.
Laughter unfurls.
A take out of the finest curry but uh ho!
'Twas too hot to handle!
Tummy feels like a well lit candle,
Rush to the loo,
Wish I never touched the vindaloo!
Bjtt feels like a funeral pyre.
Ring of fire!!

Scritch scratch wings beating against
the ceiling light.
Or
Could It be spectral nails upon the wall?
Sending goosebumps up your body.
Flickering lightbulb about to blow.
Or
Could it be a visitation letting you know...
It's there!
A movement by the window.
Shadow across the room.
Can you explain it?
So you feel a cold shiver like somebody
is walking over your grave.
Hairs standing on your neck.
Somebody watching you?
Or
Can you explain it?
Orbs of light dancing around your room.
Should you ignore it?
Or
Run?

The moon is full and round.
The sound of crickets the only sound,
In the ancient burial ground.
Not even a bark from a doggy hound.
A something reaches out from the
earthly mound.
What is happening on this night?
What is stirring?
What it is and what it might.
Hold your scream good and tight!
Your body and crunchy bones...a feasty
delight!
Eerie shadows move in the glow of the
moonlight.
Well! Don't just stand there,
Run! Run out of sight!

The heart of joy, my love.
Is watching you smile and laugh with gusto.
Makes my heart melt of the mushy kind.
My hand is encased in your shell.
Like a silken glove.
As we walk across the beach.
Sand beneath our toes.
Gentle waves lapping them in a sensual way.
I giggle at the notion of passion we lie
upon the blanket,
Serenaded by the seagulls cry.

How about you and me?
And a mug of coffee.
Or
A frothy lattè?
Sitting and chatting in a little quaint cafè
Maybe a morsel cakey bite.
Putting the world to right.
Taking time out from the madness.
Putting an end to some sadness.
A laugh would be fab!
Maybe I will pay the bill and tab
before we go stay in our hearts
for the rest of the day.

The moonbugs and trolls shall have
a blast tonight.
The goblins and fairies caught in a great
big fight.
Who shall win and who shall lose?
Douse the magic with flame and flicker!
Torch the stars with the moonshine liqueur.
All shall be quiet come the crowning dawn.
Then the toughest with brain or brawn.
Shall awake with morning breath hell!
With very sore heads!
Be quiet!
Don't yell.

Wispy white billowy whiskers graced
his weather beaten face.
A twinkling wink blasts from his azure
deep ocean eyes he spies
A flock of angels in silvery frocks.
Wearing upon their feet, no socks.
In their hands,
A harp of shimmering gold for his
ears to hark.
Heavenly music to his age old body to
relax to the max.
Stretching out upon his cloud
letting out a snore that's thundery loud!

If love

were a plant.

I would be

A timid rose

Budd.

The more

You love me.

The more I

Shall unfurl

My petals

For you!

A wise man forgot to say.
A smile and a laugh a day.
Keeps away the dismay.
Brings out the sunshine in a special way.
You know it has to be done!
So come on turn that upside down smile
the right way up and smile with the sun.

Dear window.

The light shines from the window
of your brightened eyes.
Love radiating from your soul.
Warming the very centre of me.
Envelop me with everything you have.
I give you everything I have.
From my heart and window of my soul,
I see you.
The whole of you.

Who doth dwell,
In the shadows that swell.
With the midnight moon so
full and round.
A witch's wish upon a batty bat and
owly sound.
Swish of wand with magic so wild.
Tongue of mouse and the twinkle of the moon
drops that are so mild.
Words of wisdom
Words of kind.
Words so lyrical that make earworms enter
your mind.
Wantilda Witches' cheeky grin and raucous
laughter
will lift the top of a housey rafter.
Broomstick flying in from behind her
sweeping Wantilda off her feet.
Homeward bound for a cakey treat.

One look from you
Makes my mojo steam.
One touch is a sizzle fest.
As for you kiss!
Completely undone.
You know how to capture
my rapture dude.

Here I sit upon the cold and lonely floor.
My heart, broken by your hurtful tongue.
Sobs unable to break the flow.
But I shall rise again one sunset glow.
And soar my life for somebody worthy.

First kiss when two
souls become one.
You know you are meant
to be.
Forever is destined
in that first embrace.

Oh knickers and fiddlesticks.
This wet weather is getting on my tits.
You open the door to go out,
The wind catches you in a whirly wizabout.
A cold blast straight from the arctic freezes
places that would stick out a mile!!
Knees start knocking like a deranged
crocodile.
What happened to summer this year?
Don't think we're having one this year.
Just rain, rain, rain.
Clogging Up the drain.
Sloshing up the rain.
At this rate I will turn into a toad
or grow webbed feet covered in snot!
That would be a treat...not!
Discarded inside out brollies along the
pavements here and there.
Some poking out of bushes without a care!
Holy crap sticks and pigging moly.
My boots have found a holey!
Why the hell did I come out again?
Oh yes! Off to the boot store
or buy a now boot bargain!

As I walk along the sandy shore.
The cool clear water adding serenity to my restless soul.
My feet caressed and soothed by the gentle lapping of the waves.
Froth dancing up my weary legs.
Peace creeping through my body.
I feel the warmth of the golden sun massaging the sadness and lonely solitude.
Bliss and harmony spreads through my very being.
I have come home.
My happy place.

Every morning is a new page.
Full of inspirations to paint your
mind of colour and joy.
To learn new experiences.
To walk a mile in the footsteps of
ancestors.
Do them proud and live your life.
Head held high.
You matter!

Chasing your tail.
Rushing around my feet starts to
ache and wail.
Take the kids to school.
Already frazzled but trying to stay cool.
Do your homework.
Going to work drives me berserk!
Do the shopping but fighting with a
wayward trolley.
Oh bugger it's started to rain
I forgot my brolley.
Maybe a coffee and cakey treat
in the cafe might be good.
Have a silent chuckle as you overhear
gossip from around the neighbourhood.
It has to be done!
That is good fun!
Feet are forgiving a little bit.
Rush around again realising you are no
longer so fit.
Kids, house, work, cooking, shopping.
Relax with a drink.
Do some couchy slouching
and TV flopping!

Paint a miracle in your dreams.
A full glory of technicolour I have
dreamed of you.
Spread eagled upon the blanket
on the ground
with dappled shadows of the trees dancing
over my body.
The gentle breeze playing gently with
your hair.
The sun is your smile,
Wide and bright.
Cobalt clear blue sky reflective in the
pools of your eyes.
A beautiful dream.
If only you were real.

Sometimes life feels like a
double edged sword.
Nice things going great and swell.
The people you meet along the way are kind
with soothing words.
But sometimes that can be just on the
outside with the speech from hell.

I have been wounded by the unkind,
But I have had the best of days too.
Husbands have come and gone
in and out of my mind
But I know I can't sit and wallow and stew.

The head is head is held high with
dignity and pride.
I have nothing to hide.
I am grateful for the things
I have and love you see!

HOUSE OF THE FORGETFUL MIND.

My mind has gone a little forgetful of late.
Forgive me I have forgotten your name.
Who are you again?
Hell, I forgot my own name yesterday.
Or was it the day before?
Put the washing out to dry on one of
those whatsit called.
Oh yes washing line that whizzes
about in the wind.
Forgot to bring in my knickers!
Waving about like frilly flags they were.
How the hell did I forget them?
I went for a walk and forgot to look
where I was going and noticed a
strong odour.
I am sure I didn't forget to go to the loo...
Although with my mind you never can tell!
I had trodden in dog poop.
There was both relief and a pissed off
mind as I caught sight of my shoe.
I forget what I forget now.
Never mind.

THE MENAGERIE OF THE HEART.

In my heart there's a beat with some soul.
A million thumps with gusto with a
military tattoo.
There's also a menagerie of lost loves
and tattered strings that held me together
as my heart broke.
Shards pieced together with super glue
of a new love.
A new joy to my heart.
New hopes and new dreams.

Chain
of events
lead us to
each other falling in
love.
Our hearts
beating our rhythm
for the rest of
eternity.

I didn't know the world was like this.
To wake up is always bliss.
I opened my eyes this morning
at the very start.
Full of beans and full of heart.
Full of colour and full of lust.
My heart sometimes with love would
combust.
The trees.
Waving hello or goodbye in the breeze.
People coming and going out about their day.
Whether you have warm and dry weather
or cold and wet weather.
Walking the countryside smelling the
sweet heather.
Filling your lungs with pride.
Life has ups and downs ride.
Happiness and sadness.
Goodness or badness.
The world is a beautiful but sometimes
boisterous.
Look after and fill it with grace.

Wish upon a moon for a summertime
dream.
Falling in love with a fanciful notion
of falling in love.
To feel the closeness against your skin.
To have someone to companion you
life's blunders and highs.
To laugh with
To hold with.
Someone to look into their eyes and
share
a moment of blissful love that no words are
required.
I wished upon a summertime moon
I found what I'm looking for.
My dream is coming true.
Love.
I have you!

"Lets lay that blanket on the ground!" He said
Wanting to go feral.
"It will be romantic out in the open country air
natural. "
The kissing started to warm the cockles.
She hastily undid his belt buckle.
The touching started to stir the honey pot.
They seemed to like it alot.
The buzz of flies.
The hum of bees fighting the breeze.
A fly landed on his bare butt,
And took a walk around in a bold fly strut.
She took a swipe to shoo it away.
Fly flew away without delay.
He took it as a bit of kinky and quickened
his pace.
An extra tongue took a lap on his face
A golden retriever wanted a piece of the action.
He didn't notice not even a fraction.
She noticed an audience looking on.
She started to scream but unabashedly he
carried on.

Continued from the previous page

He opened his eyes as his glory moment began.
His face went a harsh shade of reddish tan.
The audience gave a round of applause, shouts and cheers.
He and she deeply embarrassed declined to take
a bow.
The dog decided to cock his leg on him letting
out the never ending yellow wee flow.
Never again did that blanket cherish the ground.
He and she fled never again to be found.

Come hither my love.
Look above to the beckoning cloud.
Let us lie together on the lush green grass.
We could wish upon the stars and dream
of the wonders of the future that will be ours alone.
Soaring into the moonlight.
Sending each other into orbit as we make love
under the watchful night sky.
Feel the passion running through our veins.
Come and take me.
I am yours and yours alone.

Time flows through the ether.
Never standing still.
Always on the move.
All your tomorrows become today.
Today becomes your past!
The past becomes shadows in your memory.
Memories sifting into your dreams
that you want back.
People. Possessions. Life itself!
They come and they go.
Until today becomes your last!

Palm trees sway in a cloud ridden sky.
To the left.
To the right.
Then all about.
The wind picking up a right old hoolie.
Blowing leaves all over the shop.
The gentle waves out in the bay.
Turning from mild and wild,
in a blink of an eye.
Crashing about in an angry mood.
Stormy light show flashes.
Thunder overhead crashes.
Lightning whipping the skies.
The once sandy shore
littered and strewn with debris.
Cliffs pounded in full force.
Little rock pools now swallowed whole.
Devoured.
By the hungry tide.
But don't worry though!
All will be calm soon.
All will be good.
Freshened and alive in colourful
splendor once more.

Butterflies, they flutter amongst the
lavender.
Dainty in their patterned winged splendor.
Wafting wherever with not a care in the world.
Upon the breeze in the shimmery sunlit glow.
As wild as nature should be.

Shine your light with your glorious smile.
Your tender touch lights my soul on fire.
Your kiss sends me to a complete mush.
Our bodies melded together.
I am undone with desire!

I knit my fingers through yours,
We go for a stank across the land.
Up a gurt great hill as high as a mountain.
Or that's what my legs are yelling at me!
Over a granite stile we clamber.
Now! my legs are not exactly blessed with height!
Taking several moments to get over to your up
and over in a jiffy!
A path up through heather s brambles
we go.
Climbing up that bleddy steep incline.
Puffing and panting and wheezing
like a woman possessed!
We stop for a rest on a granite boulder and ponder
about stuff.
A bit of blissful kissing gets involved.
Oh! We're off again upwards.
Eventually we reached the summit.
Oh what a glorious view!
Like being on top of the world 'twas.
From the top of Trencrom Hill, turn one way
You can see the north coast, St.Ives, Godrevy,
Camborne, Carn Brea, even the mast at Four lanes.
Turning the other way, the south coast springs to view.
Mousehole, Penzance, Marazion

Continued from the previous page

and St.MIchaels Mount around Mounts Bay
to the Lizard.
We take in and marvel at this spectacular moment.
Our Cornwall!
Blessed is what we are!

You are my guiding light.
Gentle, warm and pure.
You hold me up in the dark days.
You show me what love really is.
You envelope me in your arms.
I feel safe wedged right in there.
You make my smile burst into life.
You are my love.
My joy.
My life.
My resurrection back to my whole self.
I no longer just exist.
I no longer shy away into obscurity.
I no longer feel afraid to live.
Because of you coming into my life
just when I needed you most.
I thank you with all my heart.
My body.
My soul.

Here I sit all of a daydream.
And a bowl of ice cream.
If only I had a banana to make it
a banana boat.
Feeling the soothing coolness sliding down
my throat.
Staring out of the windows sat
in an ice cream parlour booth.
What the hell!
Trying to stifle a yell.
Brain freeze I now have.
Almost braying like a calf.
Ouch that really hurts up there.
Feeling like an angry bear.
The people that I was watching are
now watching are now watching me.
Maybe I will escape to the loo
and pretend I'm going for a pee.
They might just go about their day.
Think my face has gone slightly grey.
Home time methinks.
My brain is surely on the blink.

THE BREAKUP

On my knees I shall never beg.
Don't expect for me to lower my integ.
Hurt and pain you gave constant,
Again and again you walking out
then coming back was never pleasant.
Going round in circles was dizzying.
My emotions all over the shop never
ending whizzing.
Well that bubble burst.
You dragged me through life that got
Worse.
Goodbye, farewell and all that,
I can no longer put up with all that
Crap.
Toodle pip.
Tata.
Time for me to shut that door and
Move on so you won't see me later!

I am yours and you are mine.
Life together is so sublime.
Light is dark and dark is light,
Heart in heart and hand in hand.
I melt into you at your command.
I whisper a spell of love into your ear.
The reaction is oh so clear!
Thread your love through my veins.
I shall love you forever my dear.

You hold the key to my crimson soul.
The gateway to my being.
My eternal flame burns
For your beautiful soul.

Eyes of blue,
A beautiful hue.
Dark and inviting.
Most enticing, exciting.
Drawing me in.
Hypnotising.
Completely under your spell.
Can you not tell?

I bare witness in the cave that does dwell.
Of pixies and knockers and all that
Hide from humans.
Bats and mice and all that turn at the
Blink of an eye.
Down the mineshaft long and deep.
Making mischief but do graft
With picks and with hand.
In return for a tasty pasty.

The night makes me believe in magic.
The power of darkness surrounding.
Absorbing your fears.
Eating into your soul.
Coldness creeping.
Enveloping you whole.
Look for the light.
It is a marvelous sight.
Feel and heal.
Strength you shall find from
within.

This world still talks about the time I had
a visit.
A visit from another world.
They sat at the kitchen table.
Shared a pot of tea and a hobnob they did!
They had a greenish tinge and bulging diamond
eyes that looked through you.
There was a kind of crackling noise from the
garden.
A flying thing hovering above my best petunias
That looked like a saucepan lid.
Then poof they disappeared without a trace.
Upwards into the stars and to the left.
Well I never saw them again!

The jewel of brightness
Shines from the shimmery lightness
of the sun.
Blazing with its gloryful bravado.
Cloudless azure skies blanketing the heavens.
is it any wonder how life feels alive
in the heart and the mind.
Feel good days.

Shadows calling in the darkness
from your mind.
Swirling mists mingle with your heart.
Dreams and imagination wanders the unknown
in shaky solitude.
Where do you go?
What do you do?
Do you quake and go for an ice cream fix?
Or do you man up and face your demons?

Since the day you came into my heart.
Heart jolted with a start.
Start with the morning of our meeting.
Meeting shy and pure.
Pure love started to elude.
Elude through the veins.
Veins and emotion run wild with
Want and need.
Need to be done with you always.
Always and forever.

Walk.
Don't run.
Take your time.
What's the rush?
Stop.
Look around.
Slow down.
Enjoy the scenery.

THE END.

OTHER BOOKS WRITTEN BY ME.

Poetry! Oh my days, The Poetry Collection
More Poetry by Fi.
Absolutely Bonkers.
Over The Hills and Far Away
Midnight Whispers, Lustful Poetry
The Joys of Poetry
Live, love. Laughter Poetry
Tadah! Poetic Ramblings Over
Coffee and Cake
Above And Beyond The Moon
And The Stars

Printed in Great Britain
by Amazon

13883607R00071